Your Body Never Lies

Body Language and Intuition on the Road to Enlightenment

Brian Joseph Snyder

Brian Joseph Snyder
Author

Original Copyrights 3/16 & 6/16
Brian Joseph Snyder

Third Edition
Copyright
Reverend Mike Wanner
6/15/20

Table of Contents

Foreword

I fell into this research by pushing through borders that hadn't been thoroughly examined yet. Those limitations, I found out, are not imposed upon humanity by an outside force, but rather are self-inflicted limitations on our behavior to keep us "safe."

Without spoiling the fun, I will declare that what we've kept ourselves safe from was always an illusion, made strong only by our avoidance and judgements.

And that is the beauty of this work. Because our true difficulty is self-inflicted, we already have the tools and authority to undo the sabotage that can make our life feel unworthy, "missing something," or simply just "not enough." You have the power, the strength and standing to affect this change. All you need now is a desire and a few details on how to unravel this personal lie about yourself, because you are you, and that is enough. Period.

This book is background material for The YBNL Online "Playshop," the first in the series of eight workshops. It's being released as both an introduction to YBNL and as support for "Playshop" graduates who may enjoy the fresh perspective.

To dive into the workshops, simply subscribe to and start watching the "Playshop" videos Youtube.com/freeoflimits
I'm looking forward to sharing this adventure with you!

Brian

1 - YBNL - Your Body Never Lies

"Your Body Never Lies" is a phrase that applies to body language in all of its forms. Internally, our body gives us messages via feelings and our inner voice.

We may not accurately interpret the messages all of the time, but those messages are still very valid. Externally, we use our body language to project our inner world to the universe outside of ourselves. Likewise, we continuously review others' body language to understand and interpret our present environment.

YBNL is a school for personal development that increases our intuition by improving our trust in our body and its messages. By noticing and trusting our body language cues, intuition can develop from infrequent "aha moments" into a continuous string of synchronistic events, bordering on the magical.

Yet this isn't magic. It is natural science with a grounded set of workable theories and a series of processes that reclaim stuck attention from old memories, and that allows us to be fully present, in this and any moment. Furthermore, the work only recovers the angst or emotions that appear stuck; it leaves the associated memories themselves intact.

I once had a horrible week where I lost my rental house, girlfriend, and job, all quickly. It was the trifecta of unexpected change, and I was devastated by the end of it. First, though losing my job was upsetting, it was also a relief on some level, and so was manageable stress while I considered my options.

The injustice of a broken contract angered me, as I had counted on it being fulfilled, but it also made me feel that I wasn't good enough to be wanted. But living in a large city, after all, there was bound to be something available, somewhere.

I denied the upset by setting my sights lower and taking a couple of days to recuperate before hitting the pavement. My girlfriend wanted to take me out to dinner to the latest hip spot, and we got a noisy table across the aisle from the loud bar. At the end of dinner, she said, "I'm moving to Europe," and broke up with me, no strings attached, just "goodbye."

My heart sank as I felt that I was falling in love. Was it a sense of betrayal or loss? I don't now know, but I was in shock and seemed about the size of a toothpick going home.

I had a hard time dragging myself out of bed for a couple of days, and when I did, my housemate had news. "I'm not going to renew. You can stay or go, but I'm going. Sorry."

We had four days to renew the lease or move out. My roomie was partially packed and gone the next day, and I couldn't recall feeling less wanted.

I called out for help moving and found someone to call on the last day, and so rented a truck. After a frenzy of packing and being completely exhausted, I needed help to get furniture onto the van, but when I called for the promised help, they said that they were busy and could not help, at which point I completely crashed into failure and grief.

This story, however it reads, has no more energy for me than if I told you about a lousy breakfast I had at the local diner yesterday. Whatever angst or fears or who-knows-what used to be associated with it, are now gone.

The memory is clear; There's just no energy in it. It's just pictured in my mind, in my past.

Along with a fond memory of a cat, I sat on the un-moved couch, wailing and crying my eyes out, feeling betrayed from all corners of my life when my cat jumped up on my lap and wrapped his paws around my waist for a hug. He got a smile out of me, and we stayed like that for some minutes until I stopped sobbing.

There is not a lesson to be learned here other than 1) pay attention and notice what is going on, and 2) respect and admire cats.

Before shifting my angst around those memories, though, I felt apprehension around not trusting other's commitments to me and became shy in my approach to strangers.

That wasn't any way to live. The lessons that pain taught didn't work for me, and the techniques in YBNL unraveled both the pain and the experience. All gone.

Now it's just another part of my history, I'm no longer so attached to others honoring their commitments, and I love meeting strangers. I also continue to have cats in my life.

Retraining the body not to automatically reference the past takes some work, but not decades or years. The live YBNL "Playshop," which is the core of the training, is only a two-day class.

It may be repeated, which is recommended, but it is still only 10 or 12 hours long. Considering how many years we've spent ignoring our intuition and feeling disconnected and then suffering for it, I believe that the "Playshop" is a relatively small investment of our time to get us back on track. As with anything, it does take repetition and practice and perseverance for some.

As a self-care online workshop video series, the progress can be done at your own pace.

In this first written record of the work, I review some theory and practical application of the first workshop's information.   This book does not substitute for the "Playshop": these pages are snapshots, but life and the videos are movies. What you are holding is a record of the past, while feelings and intuition only happen in the right-here right-now.

Ultimately, YBNL is about releasing the past and being fully present. There are many avenues on that journey and many perspectives from which to view them. However, there is a bigger picture, one that I could not see until I got far along in my training.

Our bodies and I mean people in general, are currently in a state of continuously (and unconsciously) referencing the past. This disconnect gives rise to all manner of problems, from attachments and resentments to fear of change and vengeful thoughts.

World culture can currently be summed up by the phrase "Hurt people hurting people." If YBNL is successful in the long term, though, this will change.

Before retraining my body, I acted out the pain of my previous story by quitting jobs without notice, dumping a girlfriend without notice, and starting preemptive arguments with housemates and family. I was in a state of expecting my past to repeat itself. Now today, I wouldn't hurt myself like that. I am not referencing my past as much, and my choices reflect it.

I can see more clearly and make better choices. The old "me" looks like a fool from here, but that is what personal growth is all about. I have grown beyond who I thought I was.

Imagine a world where we don't reference the past as a matter-of-course, but rather infrequently and by choice. Forgiveness (1) becomes more comfortable, and so does ease itself. Attachments and judgments become uninteresting, while change and expansion become more comfortable.

In the end, though, your accomplishment is for yourself. If you remember your best carefree days as a young child, then you have some idea of what life is like when we aren't carrying decades of upsets, resentments, fears, and other stresses around with us. It is liberating.

1. Forgiveness: means giving up all hope of ever having a better past.

2 - Messages

Your body always tells you the truth. Not only does it serve up information for you to process, but it also processes information itself and delivers solutions to you.

When you open your refrigerator to find something to eat, you might smell questionable leftovers to determine their viability as food. If the food smells bad, it probably is. On the other hand, if your body enjoys the smell, you will trust that information and dine away to your heart's content, this is your body telling you the truth.

YBNL is about that particular relationship we have with our body and of feeling how to reveal and cultivate awareness of our body's messages to us. Delivering this data stream of information to us is our body's job; using the information is up to us.

How we use the information, as with all choices, is partially based on free will, and partly based on the available range of information. When we increase the amount of valid information, we can make a more informed choice.

The information that we use, however, comes from two sources: the present moment (or environment), and our history and memories.

The trouble we get into is in believing that our past can help identify the present situation; we measure-and-compare our way into understanding reality. When we do it consciously, we might improve our perceptions. When our body does it unconsciously, however, we typically get into trouble.

If half of our attention is on our history or some aspect of it, we have only 50% of our focus for the present moment.

What is more real, right now? Your memories or your environment? Your memories, regardless of what else they are, are shadows of reality and are no longer happening.

Your environment, on the other hand, at this moment, is authentic and touchable.

The best possible information we can have about our present situation comes from the present moment. If we reference our past to search for similar circumstances, then we will arrive at a solution based in that history, and not based on the totality of information available to us now.

Releasing our memories (2) and leaving them in the past gives us more time for the present situation. With more attention in the present moment, we notice more information and can make adequately informed choices based on reality.

In short, releasing attention from memories gives us more time for current information.

2. Releasing our memories: means removing the emotional barbs that have hooked our attention somewhere in the past.

3 - Choices

You've never made a bad choice in your life. Every single choice and decision you've ever made was the best possible for you, based on the information you had at that time.

We all make the best possible choice for ourselves according to the information we have.

Later, after accumulating more or better information, we might think that an old choice was incorrect; this could be true based on the new data. However, we didn't have this new data back then, and therefore the new optimal choice wasn't available either. The original choice wasn't wrong; it was just based on incomplete information.

Understanding this concept is key to enjoying change without suffering because our new choices can make our old choices seem "wrong." They weren't wrong; they were appropriate at that time, and they were based on the information we had at that time.

The fact is that each choice we've ever made was the best one for us based on the information we had at that time. "Period." If we look back and see mistakes in our choices, that is an indication that we have new information and won't make the same choice again. That is "personal growth."

The process of continually upgrading our choices as we gather new information is the ideal outcome for this relationship we have with our body, which can continuously update the breadth and width of our incoming information.

One aspect of intuition training is the reclamation of attention (3) from our past to where it belongs (in-the-moment) that we might notice more information in our present environment. When we do release our hold on old memories, this doesn't erase them; it merely reduces the heavy energetic or emotional content attached to the memory.

Feeling of the memory is what distracts us from the present, it is that (the Feeling) that gets Updated. We don't change or alter our memories — that would create a layer of denial. We simply show our body that the memory is from our past and not happening now.

It truly is that simple. When our body "gets" that its stress is in the past and not happening now, our body itself lets it go. You don't have to trick, teach, hack, or otherwise coax your body into letting go; the letting go happens automatically when our body realizes that there's no longer any reason to keep holding.

The result is memory without emotional charge. The "charge" dissipates and returns as attention for our immediate use. This transformation is very quick, and the first experience of it can be quite surprising.

For one, our range of available choices opens up. Imagine if you've been shy around girls your whole life, but you just found out that your body had been reacting to an embarrassing rejection in junior high school.

If your body's response to a humiliating rejection was to become shy, then showing your body that the rejection is old and not happening anymore will also take away the reason for the shyness. This does happen; it happened to me.

When our body loses its reason for having a behavioral reaction, that reaction will go away. Typically, the heaviness of memory will go away (allowing us to feel lighter), associated behavioral patterns fall away, and new choices present themselves to us.

One thing about filters (4) and blinders (5) is that we do not know what they are masking. If we did know that agents-of-denial wouldn't be good at their job, would they?

The removal of our filters and the opening of our blinders will allow more information to get through to us. With this new information, our range of choices will increase and improve. In turn, the latest information can make our old choices appear wrong, misguided, foolish, not good enough, bizarre, or even emotionally childish. While the assessment may be valid from our current perspective, it needs to be understood as evidence that we have grown and will not make the same mistakes again.

Getting the body to let go of its patterns (by correcting the body's perception of an event's location in time) is not healing. It is simply a shift in perception that retrains the body to notice when events are real (happening now) vs. unreal (happened in the past).

The real healing happens outside of class and outside of training when we are again confronted with old situations. If our body has genuinely shifted, new information and new choices will be available to us. Picking a new choice solidifies any gains made and is itself the actual healing.

3. Filters: The body's information-sanitation system. We filter incoming information by measuring & comparing it to what we already "know."
4. Filters: The body's information-sanitation system. We filter incoming information by measuring & comparing it to what we already "know."
5. Blinders: The body's tools to ensure denial.

4 - Body Language

The jewel of YBNL is a simple fact that we created our body language. You have the authority to change or recreate it by it being yours.

If you rent your house, then you probably don't have permission (or a desire) to remodel it. If you own your home, however, then you perhaps seek to continually upgrade it, at least until it meets your standards of aesthetics and comfort.

Own your body; it is yours. You organized it, you furnished it, and you can choose when to clean it up and when to remodel it.

Anything in the house you don't like? Are there monsters in the basement? Is there trash piling up? Own it, and you don't need permission to clean it up, you can just take care of it.

All we require to change our body's language is:

- an understanding of how we created it
- a willingness to be responsible (6) for it
- tools to transform, release or otherwise change it

The first item, identifying the cause, is simple: it is your past unwillingness to experience an unpleasant event. It is something you did, and it is also something you failed to do. The good news is that you can shift or change it.

When life throws at us something we either can't or don't want to experience, we psychically push it away. Whether we call it denial, avoidance, or self-preservation, the effect is the same. We get to not-feel (and otherwise not perceive) whatever is happening, and our body holds on to it for later.

The emotions are pushed into our body and get stored as physical tension. On the other hand, the mental aspect splits off and rests in mind, though generally not quietly.

This result, of now continually holding on, gets added to the body language we project to others. Whether it be judgments, personal issues, fears, or otherwise, it's all in our body's tension, and it does get responded to, consciously or not.

The solution is simple; we return the two halves into one. We are merely reversing the process. How this is accomplished is by locating tension in the body and identifying its correlating old event or issue by reading body language.

When the halves are restored, our body very quickly recognizes that the event isn't currently happening and is only a memory. Tension is released (from both mind and body) as well as its resulting body language, both internal and projected. Our body itself disappears the stress into memory; our job is simply to bring the two parts back into one

The entire process, once the physical or emotional stress has been reunited with its story or issue, can take under a second. It can be near-instantaneous and sometimes can take up to a minute for the connection and relief to occur. If the release does not happen in seconds, then we probably haven't found the right context yet.

That is the entire process. We reconnect the mental memory of the suppressed event or issue with its correlating emotional part. Reconnection is accomplished when trainees internally feel the indicated area of their body while recalling the associated situation. "Recalling" could be anything from flashes of images or emotions to mild reflection, and isn't different from remembering except that it can happen very fast.

Our body takes care of the rest, releasing the event to memory. This discontinuation of holding on returns energy and attention to us, as we are no longer distracted by a story.

Epiphanies usually follow one hour to two weeks after a resolution and relief. When life presents itself in new ways and with new choices, indicating that something has been released, shift happens.

It took me many years of facilitating private training to realize that our body believes that our old unresolved issues and traumas are still happening. That is the reason for physical stress.

When we reconnect body sensations with old memories, the body recognizes that the event is a memory and puts it in its proper place: the past. The reason for holding on is over, and the issue is let go.

It truly is this simple. It isn't always easy, but it is this simple.

Put another way (in five steps):

1. You refused to feel something,
2. and instead stuck it in your body,
3. which is now continually feeling it for you.
4. When you are willing to reconnect with it,
5. your body will simultaneously offer it up and disappear it into memory.

The YBNL "Playshop" disentangles the first two steps and examines the source of the body's desire to hold on. Partnered exercises give a grounded experience of change, as we enjoy the transformation as both individuals and as a group.

It's impossible to share the core "Playshop" information here, however. Books are, by their nature, collections of thoughts. The "Playshop" is about Feeling, and the bridge, between the thinking and the Feeling, can't be crossed on paper, at least not by my hand.

The third step is to feel unresolved events for us continually, is explained in this book. Now we can understand what it is we are shifting, and why.

The fourth and fifth steps are facilitated in private training until old stress is being released on its own. Individual work can't exist on paper, though. While I may be happy to explain the mechanical theory, no matter what I write, you can't get live, in-person training from a book.

As far as what to do first, neither private training nor the group workshop is better than the other: they are two sides of the same coin. On the one hand, we hone in on personal issues to teach the body the value of letting go. On the other side, we learn the underlying mechanics and not take matters personally.

A third route, a video series presented as self-care, is also available. Links to The YBNL Online "Playshop" can be found at YourBodyNeverLies.org.

As in everything, the recommendation is always to do what feels right when it feels right.

6.: Responsibility: Means "respond with your abilities," it doesn't mean credit or blame.

5 - Good News

After performing hundreds of sessions and witnessing the transformations that can and do occur, I've come to several conclusions. By my observation, they appear to work as theoretical models for the results that YBNL achieves.

1. Because we get relief when our body stops holding on to old stories, the holding-on must be creating the issue. The story itself is no longer creating discomfort; it ended being real a long time ago. Holding-on is (was) creating the trouble, in all cases.

The Excellent News is that we don't have to relive our stories to release the stress. Drama doesn't release trauma because the story isn't the issue. Holding-on is creating the problem, not what we are holding to.

YBNL isn't therapy; we don't tell or listen to stories. We're just training our bodies to be here now and to stop holding-on.

2. If the holding on created the discomfort, then letting go should (and does) dissipate the pain. And what we hold on with is attention; our attention on the issue is how we hold.

Excellent news, for many reasons. First, attention isn't something you have to look for and find – it is closer than any "thing." Second, it means that letting go will return the dividend of increased awareness for our present environment now.

We are merely taking attention from the past (now no longer real) and bringing in the present (to more fully be here).

3. Angst, pain, fear, a sense of emptiness, of loneliness. No matter how you slice it or label it, it is stuck attention. The event has flavored what it is stuck to, but it is still just attention, focused on something that is no longer happening. It is our attention transformed from free will in the present moment into stuck energy-in-the-past.

Our stuck attention is available to be reclaimed. Furthermore, retrieving our focus from old events transforms the discomfort.

One of my definitions of attention is the "capacity to take outside information in." The more awareness we have available, then the more we notice from outside of ourselves. The less attention we have, then the less information we see.

From a survival perspective, it seems better to have more information from which to base our choices, and that is the point: when we reclaim stuck attention from our past, we can then make better choices in the present.

Because our denials and blinders are all different from others' blinders and contradictions, we cannot foreshadow what gains might be made by releasing attention from specific old events. In other words, we can't predict what relief or expansion a particular person will receive from a release. We may all be cut from the same cloth, but we've all worn it in our own way.

For myself, I find that there is always more to see and release, but along the way, I've had some good ones. For one, my perception of color has drastically improved; one day, I suddenly noticed thousands of shades of green in the forest, where before I had seen only dozens. It has made nature far more entertaining, especially on hikes through the woods.

My ability to talk to strangers has dramatically improved, to the point where I've shocked more than a few of my friends by starting conversations with random people. Compared to my past shyness, this milestone has freed me to make new friends much more quickly, and also to cut away from those whom I no longer feel comfortable.

Those are two examples of how my body now uses the attention that had been stuck on old events. I don't recall what those events were, though, as they don't matter anymore.

6 - Shift Happens

The body holding onto unresolved events creates all manner of conditions, all of which are resolved instantaneously after the body lets go.

An unresolved event is still happening right now, from our body's perspective, and it tenses in response. Reconnecting the tension to the memory (or thoughts of the event) shows the body that the thing is old and no longer happening.

In most cases, that is all the body needs to know. If an event is no longer real, then there is no need for resolution – there is no problem to be solved.

That's it. It truly is that simple. Getting there might not always be easy, but it is still that simple.

What is complicated is the litany of ramifications as we, in the present moment, attempt to deal with our body's need to resolve something that we've entirely forgotten. It's an awkward situation, to be sure.

We end up trying to solve problems that don't exist or ignoring ones that do. We suffer for what was, and we don't experience what could've-been. We get triggered, and out comes the anger, or rejection, or shame (we all do it differently). Sometimes we might behave appropriately for an old event, but not for the present moment (easier to see in others than ourselves).

I label the effects of trauma into three separate categories: blinders, filters, and patterns. They each have their unique character and also their reward for resolution.

Blinders prevent us from seeing something, usually a circumstance but sometimes individuals or groups of people. For example: if we've been rejected for jobs frequently and repeatedly by blond, female human-resource authorities, we might develop blinders that prevent us from interacting with blond females in social settings. We might not see them as friendly or approachable, and so just ignore them.

They are called blinders because they cause blind spots – in this case, any new information about blond females is shut down. We don't want to see them, we don't want to hear about them, and we certainly don't want to interact with them in a way that would make us feel further rejected.

Rejection feels awful, certainly worse than blinders, and so the body determines that blinders are a better option. It is a kind of ignorance (7) we can have, and it dramatically reduces our range of choices.

If a blond were to come up to us and we were experiencing our filters, we would not hear what she says. Rather than taking her at face value, we would filter and interpret her words to fit our blinder.

The attractive woman says, "I enjoy classical music," and in our head, we hear, "you can't keep up with me."

The third category of latent tendencies are behavioral patterns, hidden and outside of our control. These are programs that predetermine how we act in certain situations. While under a program's influence, we simply play the part and are unaware of what is happening. Only once complete do we notice that we've been playing out an old pattern.

How many times have we sworn "never to do that again" only to realize later that we have "done it again?"

Our patterns exist to work out stressful situations; once the stress diminishes, we can notice that we did replay a program. So we promise again. If it happens enough times, or if the behavior gets us into trouble, we might examine the pattern, which can lessen its strength.

Truly ending old habits, though, requires showing our body that the situation, which gave rise to the practice, is no longer happening. That is the long and short of it.

It's Good News that this work takes away the body's need to replay old situations. After all, if they are old, then there is no reason for the body to address them, right?

Blinders, filters, behavioral patterns all vanish when their cause is released. However, this isn't the goal of YBNL. The purpose of YBNL is an increase in intuition and present-time awareness. To that end, the removal of obstacles that prevent us from being here now is essential, for intuition only happens in the present; we don't get messages yesterday or tomorrow.

As our attention is reclaimed, it converts from being stuck in the past to being attachment-free in the present.

Our blinders open up, and this is "results telling the truth": if attention has been reclaimed, then we should be noticing more information in our environment.

7. Ignorance: means "Ignore this."

7 - Intuition

YBNL addresses three kinds of intuition, which I've labeled as personal, familiar, and universal. The first arises from our life experiences and is based on our certainties – it's how we apply our knowledge and training, and it is how we know what to say or do next when we aren't thinking. It comes purely from within us.

A competent doctor with decades of diagnostic experience might be able to identify disease by a glance at our complexion and odor. In contrast, an intern would need to run blood and urine tests, then look in our eyes and tongue and then double-check everything.

Another example might be a mechanic who knows what is wrong with our car by its exhaust noise alone. Or an experienced stockbroker might make choices based on long-term charts, without being able to identify what he sees in those charts.

This type of information can be stifled quickly by our inner critic. Personal intuition requires a level of certainty that not everyone can achieve without training; for most of us, denying our intuition is far more comfortable than acting upon it. For this reason, we tame our inner critic as part of our initial intuition training[8].

How often have we known what was going to happen next, but didn't realize it until after the event had passed? We'll then exclaim, "I knew it!" and wonder why we didn't respond while it still mattered.

With attentiveness and repetition, we can train ourselves to stop and listen when intuitive information comes to us, and this is another example of "your body never lies."

"Familiar intuition" comes from our friends and family, our teammates and our coworkers and is dependent upon how close we feel to them. Pure intuition arises from repeated interactions with others; it appears to depend upon emotional connection and physical proximity, though not always.

Example: we think about calling a friend we haven't heard from in days and then immediately our phone rings, and it's them calling us. Group sports also enjoy a degree of this; as spectators, we can see how cohesive teams respond intuitively tend to beat less-cohesive ones.

Another example: one time, I walked into my girlfriend's kitchen and heard her ask me to get ice cream. I called out to the living room, "What flavor do you want?" to which she exclaimed, "I didn't even ask you out loud!" These synchronicities are shared amongst the well connected.

This natural intuition can appear to be magical, but it is really "par for the course." When we feel connected, we are connected, by definition.

Being connected involves sharing information; if we are not sharing information, then how do we feel connected? We can't and don't.

Connection requires sharing, and sharing requires a connection. Natural intuition is the result of having a meaningful, connected relationship.

Natural intuition can be proof that we are genuinely connected.

Intuition naturally increases and expands as our comfort levels, and connections grow. The expansion of this category of intuition occurs as we increase our ability to connect with others (9).

The third I call "universal" as it can come from any location and by any means; it has no regard for distance, or the laws of physics, perhaps. The information can be completely random and without an obvious source. It can also be sought and tamed, though; techniques for accessing universal intuition turn magic into science (10).

When we hit this stage of connection, life performs synchronicities that verify our connection (11). Just this week, I was looking to feel inspired to finish this book and was drawn into a thrift store. The first thing I see, staring at me in the foyer, is an empty picture frame with a quote for decoration. It reads:

"Do something
that nobody else has done,
something that will dazzle the world."

Of course, I bought it, and it now sits on the table where I write. That's an example of universal intuition telling me where to go to have my desire fulfilled; I sought inspiration and intuition delivered.

I've now written as much in three days as I have in the previous month, and I get to glance at the inspirational words if ever my energy feels low (12).

This story isn't so unusual, it just so happens to be relatively recent and relevant. The Feeling or sense of connection we develop naturally produces synchronistic events, and it isn't just for the high-born or anointed or chosen; it is available to anyone (13).

When we've tamed and retrained our inner critic, and after we've learned the physics of connecting, and then gained some certainty after practice and repetition of the exercises, universal intuition becomes another method with which to understand and interact with the world.

While a picture may be worth a thousand words, an experience can be worth a thousand stories. So rather than fill this book with stories, I aim to inspire you to get trained and to have your own experiences. Besides, this training is relatively short(14); it'd be faster just to do the workshops than to listen to a bunch of wild tales.

⸸

8. The "Playshop" helps to silence our inner critic and to be here now.
9. Techniques are taught in both the EnergyWorks and Night School workshops.

10. Intuition and manifestation appear to be two sides of the same coin.
11. For now, I've left the picture frame empty.
12. For now, I've left the picture frame empty.
13. Everybody is different, and the results do vary by the body. As external influences will slow, delay, or impede results, participants are asked to be free and clear of foreign substances to the best of their ability.
14. The entire YBNL training schedule is eight workshops spread out over a minimum of one year to allow for practice, integration, and repetition as necessary. Additional coaching and teacher training are also available.

8 - Filters

To increase our intuition, we need only remove the filters[4] that mask it.

I once believed that intuition was a skill that could be learned in the same way that one might learn archery; through patience and practice. When that didn't go far, I considered to approach it the way I'd learn a trade; through study and hands-on experience with experts willing to teach. However, that wasn't much help, either. Intuition is just too close.

I adopted another perspective; that intuition is already perfect. Training then became not about intuition, but about listening to it. It seems so simple on its face yet wasn't so apparent to me for a long time. Intuition, I came to realize, starts with noticing what is. I had to unlearn the habits that masked and invalidated my perceptions.

I deduced that expectations were overlaying reality, taking my attention away from the present. Rather than merely noticing the obvious, I was running commentary in my mind about what I thought was happening. Granted, I didn't fully see this until I'd learned to be still and quiet, but we've certainly all experienced this to some degree or another.

It appears that conscious tendencies (filters) coupled with unconscious ones (underlying patterns and blinders) together manifest a self-created virtual reality. This "reality," based partly on the current environment and partly on our history, is a world of comparison and identification.

Referencing the past creates the appearance of a familiar world, but our history populates it; it is an appearance only. It can be comforting at times, but it isn't here now. It is here then.

The primary filters we unravel to find our intuition are:
- Judging
- Measuring & Comparing
- Caring what others think

Ownership of our experience gives us control of those tools: after all, it is us who judges, us who measures & compares, and it's us who identifies with the suffering that follows.

Our filters, the lenses through which we interpret reality, are precisely that: ours. What a relief! If we own them, we can shift them.

All we need do to remove our filters is to choose otherwise, and then re-choose when we catch ourselves filtering again. Eventually (habits can take weeks to shift), filtering will no longer be automatic.

Judging as to "good" or "bad" requires referencing the past. We see something that we don't understand and then look into our memories to make sense of it. Judging takes us out of the present moment as we make the relevant associations. Even if we believe that we understand, it is impossible to know all the facts and circumstances that lead to someone else's personal choice. To make sense of it, we conclude from experiences in our past.

Labeling as good or bad creates a disconnection between our self and our target; pointing out something itself creates separation, as in "look how we are different."

On top of all this, the past we reference is our own. It is our memories that provide the basis for the judgment; therefore, who we are genuinely judging is our self.

Reasons to give up Judging:
- it pulls us into our past
- it creates disconnection
- it prevents us from feeling unconditional love

Judging others prevents us from feeling unconditional love, so even in this way, we lose presence(15). Also, judging others is a choice. It may have become a habit or an addiction, but it is still a choice at its core.

The other filters are, in some ways, subsets of Judging. We must measure & compare when we collect evidence to judge. "Caring what others think" is simply a concern for their judgments about us. However, once we realize that our judgments have no power outside of ourselves, we tend to drop that concern.

Imagine how much attention you could have freely available if your mind didn't waste time judging this, that and them. Instead, you could be noticing how amazing it is to have a body and to be alive. Right now is a pretty awesome time just to be!

15. Charisma might be a function of unconditional loving-ness.

9 - Cleaning House

The process of resolving our past is very much like cleaning house: the obvious messes get noticed and tidied up first.

When we clean up, we might start by doing the dishes and cleaning the counters. Once that is done, then we notice that dusting is a priority. Only after dusting do we notice the filth on the windows, so we clean those inside and out. Upon returning inside, we see the need to vacuum, do it, and then we remember to take out the trash.

As we clean up our house: we take out the deadweight (trash), open the curtains, let the sun in, and feel better about life and living there.

Cleaning happens in layers, and so does our resolution of longstanding issues.

Each layer (or issue) peeled away and released also diminishes or clears its associated filters, blinders, and patterns. Our awareness expands, and those blinders no longer blind us, and the filters no longer mask "what is." Then, another issue or forgotten event comes into view, just like cleaning the house.

We continue noticing what we need to take care of until either: our house is spotless, we are exhausted, or until we feel that it is "clean enough." It is up to us.

YBNL goes a step further, however, bringing a new possibility into view. What if cleaning our house taught the house how to clean itself?

That is what we are doing: we are teaching our body the value of not holding on and also a method of letting go.

The repetition of letting go teaches our body the value of not holding on. Eventually, our bodies will 'get it.' In this way, the training is more like riding a bicycle; once our body gets it, letting-go can become second nature, happening in the background.

When our body understands the process and feels the benefit, it will begin reclaiming attention on its own and also will not hold onto impactful memories in the first place.

You only need bicycle lessons until your body "gets it," and then you can ride freely. Likewise, we only do private training until our body "gets it" and begins releasing emotional hooks and anchors on its own.

The result is a body that processes and releases stressful events as they happen. Last year I had to flee the Valley Fire, which consumed our rental home two minutes after I left it. I lost all of my clothes and shoes, music, computer, collectibles, books, jobs, and on and on. Three weeks later, my girlfriend and I were at emergency services, looking to sign up for aid and assistance.

"What was your address again?" "Where were you living?" "And you lost your house?" "What was that address?" After more than a few suspicious looks, we realized that we didn't have the same upset and grief that other victims had. To get through the process, we feigned sadness and nodded our heads longingly when folks would tell their stories.

Our visits continued until the melancholy just got too dull; two months after the fire, I felt like enough was enough – the sadness expected of me was a debt that wasn't worth paying for clothing and food handouts.

While I empathize with other disaster victims who continue to feel traumatized, I also know that it isn't the event itself that is causing current discomfort. It's the body holding on, believing that the trauma is still happening.

I am eternally grateful to have trained my body in this way, before the fire. It was quite an eye-opener to witness the difference in responses to the trauma and was a catalyst to get me onto writing this book.

Clean this house (temple), and it will maintain itself (clarity).

10 - Access

Most of us don't recognize our intuition until its usefulness has passed. Therefore, the first step to expanding and increasing our full intuition is to untangle it. I use the term "untangle" because our perception of it has been tangled with that of our inner critic.

I grew up with a pool table in a rec room and spent hundreds of hours attempting near-impossible shots by calculating the angles defined by the diamond markers between the holes. After some months, I found myself noticing the correct aspects without having to do the calculations. That is personal intuition, trained into existence. My inner critic, however, would sometimes argue with what seemed like the correct choice. Whether or not the argument was valid, it seemed that merely having attention on the critic would be enough to miss the shot.

Before taking action, our inner critic can debate our plan, the merits, or even the future results of our effort. If we get beyond that stage, then while the action is being taken, the critic can return to sabotage the results (and prove its earlier argument).

If you've played pool before then, you'll probably recognize this story: we go to take a shot and then, just before striking the cue ball, we know that we are going to miss. We take the chance anyway (and miss) and then say something like, "I knew it!" That is personal intuition, but it's also the critic getting in the way of our choices and our success.

Discerning between the two is simple, though not always easy—basically, our intuition whispers, and our ego screams. The loud voice is either attempting to prevent change or prove a negative. The quiet voice is trying to nudge us in the right direction. One key to discerning between the two is to create time to do so.

In our example above, the loud voice says, "It's gonna miss!" as we swing the stick towards the cue ball. There is a time gap between hearing the sound and hitting the ball, and within that gap is a chasm. The chasm is between the choices of continuing (and missing) or stopping (and reevaluating our aim). Ignore the time-gap, and it passes quickly. Examine it, however, and you'll find it to be broad and full of all manner of habits and patterns.

It can be challenging to stop a losing momentum, and not just at games. How many times have you been frustrated by this? Don't take it personally (there isn't anything "wrong" with you) as everyone goes through it to some degree. But recognize it as it happens, and you can stop and wait to take your shot until you know that you will be successful.

The chasm is also the distance between living a life in-the-past and living in-the-moment. When we are here now, there is no loud voice, and there is no gap, just a clean shot, and success.

The YBNL "Playshop" crosses that chasm by examining and dissecting the critic, not to destroy it but to retrain it. While the critic can appear to be an inevitable aspect of being human, that is not the case. It is our inner body language, and its job is to keep us not only alive but also to protect aspects of life that we deem essential. It can be trained to accomplish its goals with other means; however, just as a temper-tantrum-throwing child can learn different ways of getting their desires met.

Competitive threats to self-esteem or social standing, or only competition itself, can trigger the critic into action. In the "Playshop," we give our inner voice better tools with which to do its job, turning it from a sabotaging critic into a guard that watches our back. The accomplishment will take some practice, and results do begin immediately during the class.

Towards the result of an expanded intuition, we'll need to give up habits and patterns that have caused us to ignore or deny it in the past. Lucky for us, it appears that the critic and our latent tendencies are interrelated; they cannot exist independently of each other.

This field's genius lies herein, for there is a direct correlation between our external body language (what others see) and our inner body language (the critic or otherwise). In other words, our bodies never lie.

In YBNL, we exploit this quickly; partnered exercises that bring awareness to our external body language also modify our internal voice by bringing it into our awareness.

11 - Private Training

In the chapter "Body Language," I listed out the five steps of creating and dissipating unresolved issues in our past. They are:

1. We refused to feel something,
   and instead stuck it in our body,
   which is now continually feeling it for us.
2. When we are willing to reconnect with it,
   our system will simultaneously offer it up
   and it will disappear into memory.

YBNL private training is facilitated repetition of the 4th and 5th steps, repeated to the point of teaching the body to let go on its own. This transformational learning needs to be repeated a few times.

The first time we were able to get up on a bicycle, our mind raced with calculations for balance, steering, and pedaling. Once our body "got" how to ride a bike, however, we could then move, steer, and keep our balance without thinking. Transformational learning shifts how our body understands and interacts with the outside world, in our example, a bicycle.

When we can ride the bicycle, then our training is over; our perspective has been transformed, and the training wheels come off. Results "tell the truth"; either we can ride the bike or we can't.

In this vein, YBNL training is considered complete when our body begins to let go of old tensions on its own.

Furthermore, the outcome of the training is the ability to release old stress whenever it appears, allowing us to "be here now" more fully. This skill improves and becomes second nature with personal practice, just as bicycle riding skills can improve with practice.

A quick study in most instances (six to ten sessions), though meetings are best spaced two weeks to a month apart.

It generally takes two weeks to grow accustomed to new habits (or the lack of old ones) and to feel grounded in a new way of seeing the world. Without the benefit of the YBNL "Playshop," though, trainees should wait another two weeks before their next training session.

Fifteen years ago, I was talked into working on a friend-of-a-friend, 'Sally,' whose body was locked up in the shoulders and chest. She wasn't told about the body language aspect of the work, only that she would "feel better." Whoops. I learned more than a few lessons about comfort levels, but it all ended well.

I don't recall the issues or memories released, but her shoulders relaxed, and her solar plexus lost its knot. When I was finished, she started crying and said I should leave. I got home to find out that she'd called and yelled at my girlfriend for not telling her what I was going to do. I felt awful.

My first thought was that I'd never work on anyone for free again, as payment is a good indication that someone knows what they are getting and why. As I pondered the upset, I had a sinking feeling that Sally felt violated and that I'd let myself be cast in the role of "therapist."

As a trainer or facilitator teaching someone how to retrain their own body, any perceived mistakes or errors can be easily (and lightly) addressed. However, once the facilitator is on the therapist pedestal, the trainee has given authority and responsibility to them, making any further adjustments difficult, "heavy" and improbable.

The trainee is doing the letting-go; their body is the expert (or expert-in-training), not the facilitator. The facilitator's job is one of service; if they turn into "the expert," the organic balance of power will shift, and the trainee's body will then refuse to feel connected.

There was nothing I could do as Sally was convinced that remembering whatever-it-was was causing her upset. However, I had seen her body let it go. I had to stand back and wait. A week went by. Then two. In the middle of the third week, I got a call from her.

"Thank you so much! I hung out with my Mom all weekend, and we were best friends like when I was a kid!" I was incredibly grateful to get that call and hear the report, and to then sleep better again.

I, of course, learned a lot about what I do, and about what I don't do anymore. The most solid lesson was confirming the adjustment time.

I've seen it many times since: a private training session appears ineffective or uninspiring, but a couple of weeks go by, and then an excellent report comes in.

I stress the value of making new choices when new options present themselves. For if we have truly let something go, that implies that its associated filters and blinders are also gone.

Giving more attention to the current moment can improve our range of perception. Shift happens when we notice and make new choices.

Creating new choices confirms our unique perceptions and anchors our gains. This aspect of private training may take weeks to set in, but it can shift quickly with attentiveness.

"Playshop" graduates may space their private training one to two weeks apart according to their comfort level. Because the workshop addresses the mechanics of why we hold on, graduates tend to remain grounded during their adjustment period and may train more frequently.

I have never facilitated training for anyone more than ten times. Once the body "gets it" and begins releasing attention from old events on its own, facilitated sessions feel like training wheels on a bicycle – in the way and slowing us down.

12 - Time

One thing about the expansiveness of this work is that we begin to notice new information and also begin making new connections to old data. A natural result of having fewer distractions in our mind; our attention is free to examine the matters at hand without overlaying any early experience from our past.

Many misconceptions I've noticed are cultural (perhaps that's obvious, as universal ones should be excessively rare in nature). From the perspective of this work, one glaring error in our thinking is the belief that "time heals all wounds." It is complete nonsense and based not on healing but rather on forgetting.

Time doesn't heal wounds. It will help us go numb to the memory, perhaps, but that isn't healing. It turns out that time, through the action of burial, numbing, and forgetting, actually increases the strength of old wounds.

When we forget about a wound, it festers in the background and generates filters, blinders, and underlying patterns, all created as coping mechanisms by our subconscious. Our body (or psyche) believes that our unresolved traumas are still happening, right now, and it behaves appropriately.

Blinders ultimately prevent us from perceiving similar situations, while filters alter our perceptions just enough to avoid activation of our dramatic response.

If our filters can't mask the situation and if our blinders aren't active or healthy enough to prevent engagement, then our unconscious patterns will kick in.

We never notice these subconscious activities while they are happening, precisely because they are not in our consciousness. When our pattern is over, however, that is when we notice it.

How many times have you caught yourself doing something that you swore you would never do again? How many times have you promised yourself that you wouldn't make those same poor choices again? Probably more times than you can count, otherwise this material wouldn't interest you, nor would you have reason to investigate this phenomenon.

If time healed our wounds, then our subconscious wouldn't need these methods of avoiding similar situations; you would simply lead your life and continuously make new, upgraded choices as you gain further information from your experiences.

This method of coping with the present by unconsciously referencing the past is something we learned in the classroom of life, as it appeared to be the only option available. But that is no longer the case. You can train yourself to experience the present fully, without referencing similar situations in your past, and the results can be quite magical.

Amazingly, the training is not only comfortable but also fun in the sense that the practice itself is one of repeated relief. As you give your body experiences of release and relief from past upsets, your body will notice the benefit and will learn how to let the old stuff go on its own in the background.

It's very much like riding a bicycle after falling a few times. If someone can hold your weight and keep the bike steady while you adjust your sense of balance, very quickly, your body will "get" that balancing the bike is better than falling over. Once you can repeat balancing the bike on your own a few times, your body will feel how to do it – you will no longer have to think about it.

Personal training works the same way: a facilitator helps you locate and resolve an old issue, which gives your body experience of release. After noticing the benefits and repeating it a few times, your body "gets it," and further releases become relatively effortless.

13 - Drama

The goal of YBNL is the development of an intuition bordering on the magical. To this end, we release our hold on old traumas, we discontinue referencing our past, and we learn to stop and listen when intuition whispers.

The old model of "healing," generally based on the sharing of traumatic stories in a group, followed by emotive transformation through breathing or other means, does not lend itself to our goal.

While some relief can be felt through that type of work, it isn't the same as letting go. The churning of old trauma, and "really getting in there" to examine the details, is akin to sifting through our trash when cleaning the house. It's already been thrown in the garbage, so why go through it again and risk making a mess?

In YBNL, we simply take the trashcan to the curb; we don't sift through it first.

Put another way: "the past can't tell you who you are, only who you were." But who you were no longer exists, so why bother? Everything you are is right now.

Drama doesn't release trauma; it recycles it. Emoting old stories does not release us from them. In some ways, the stories get "locked in." I've been to too many workshops and healing circles where folks are replaying and regurgitating the same stories over and over, believing that they are slowly peeling layers away.

Perhaps they are. However, they are also creating repetition, which our bodies love. The repetition creates a feeling of safety and can, in some cases, create an addiction to emotive (or dramatic) therapies.

The past can't tell us who we are, only who we were, and who-we-were no longer exists. Besides, it isn't the past giving us trouble; it's the holding-onto-it that is.

14 - Escape

Alcohol and other drugs create filters, blinders, and patterns.

Unresolved events create subconscious programs from within organically (though not necessarily), drugs, whether humanmade or not, are synthetic creators of experiences, feelings, and blinders & filters.

These can temporarily ease the suffering of activated traumas. Still, they can create new drama and heaviness, directly (by harming the body) and indirectly (e.g., by producing misunderstanding, fear, or avoidance).

A substitution of synthetic feelings for our organic feelings is not healing; it is a temporary escape that perpetuates itself. After all, who wouldn't want to eat / smoke / drink something that makes them "feel better?" With a little repetition, our body can quickly notice that synthetic life feels better than our organic one, and so will follow that path.

The problem is that the organic one doesn't go away; the synthetic experience overlays the organic one, and so now there are two.

Imagine a character stepping into a virtual reality machine. Now imagine them having been in there long enough to forget where they are. The computer-generated world appears "real."

They find themselves feeling lost and start looking for familiar landmarks. A sense of disconnection comes over them when they realize they are all alone. They start walking in hopes of finding a friendly face, and after some traveling, find a smiling salesman offering to ease the pain.

"Just put on these virtual reality goggles, and you can be in a better world."

Now our protagonist puts on the new goggles, and begins believing the next virtual reality; they forget that the second one isn't real either. They not only forget about the first, uncomfortable virtual world, but they get far removed from their organic reality, sitting in a chair somewhere with real, physical goggles on. If we were to pull the authentic glasses off, our character might have a heart attack or a psychotic episode. It can become a lot to unravel.

Drugs and alcohol get in the way of this work in the same way, by their nature. YBNL is the opposite of escape. We seek reality and to "take our goggles off," so to speak. To this end, we minimize our consumption of affective substances.

YBNL training, both the workshops and facilitated private training, require that participants be drug and alcohol-free for a minimum of 24 hours before participation. Though I've seen results get impacted by synthetics taken 72 hours prior, the bulk of the effects wear off faster than that, and so the compromise.

Long term, chronic users of substances, however, need to be free of their addictions before starting training. Social users just need to take a break, in most cases.

15 - Light

Enlightenment isn't a place; it is a process. It is the process of lightening up.

When our latent tendencies get triggered, a predetermined program gets played out. Later, after it has run its course, we'll suddenly realize that we've yet again acted according to an old script, despite our previous promises. It can be incredibly frustrating.

These scripts we play out can be quite dramatic, especially if we feel our life, wealth, or standing are under threat. That isn't any fun, and it is heaviness.

Resolving old traumas and issues removes our body's need to create the associated filters, blinders, and scripted patterns. They simply go away. There isn't any need to "fix," "rewrite," "cope with," or otherwise change the tendencies, as they are gone. Eventually, as our body resolves and reclaims attention on its own accord, clarity and ease reveal themselves.

Discarding our old, oppressive tendencies lightens the weight we feel in our body. This is "Results telling the truth" – As when we let go of something heavy or substantial, we should feel less weight.

An exciting piece of YBNL is the correlation between feeling lighter and having expanded mental space. It seems that "lighter" doesn't only mean less weight (e.g., on the shoulders), but it also means being able to take things lightly.

As our patterns fall away and our attention is reclaimed, we not only notice more information in our immediate environment, but we also become more willing to let it be. We can find ourselves with more room for empathy and understanding.

Our old need to "be right" or to "fix" the outside world is no longer there, leaving open space or an allowance in its wake. In this way, we take ourselves lightly and can rest easy, knowing that we have lightened up. Shift happens.

16 - Wrap Up

Five years of handwritten and laptop notes, and the working manuscript for "<u>Your Body Never Lies</u>," were lost to the Lake County, California Valley Fire of 2015.

Fire doesn't make mistakes (it just is.) This work, though a bit dense with information, reads easier and flows in much more gentle ways than my previous attempt. Please don't mind the repetition – the multiple perspectives on the same data appear to help the live learning process ("Playshop" graduates will recognize the circular route). I believe that it helps in book learning as well. We'll see.

Rereading the book might help ground the information if you catch yourself trying to believe it. Of course, seeing it live is probably the best way to find out if this information works. You can see our schedule or sign up for the newsletter at yourbodyneverlies.org, where you will also find links to video workshops.

This edition is meant as a support structure for The YBNL "Playshop," both live and the online videos. I honor your patience with me as I know the book has been a long time coming.

This information is part of the guru-free system. It doesn't mean that we are against gurus (I have sat at the feet of many and love them all), it just means that we come to YBNL for the information, not the facilitators.

Currently, The YBNL School for Personal Development hosts workshops online as well as coaching and free Q & A sessions. You may begin the 'Your Body Never Lies' Online "Playshop" at any time.

As in everything, the recommendation is always to do what feels right when it feels right. I hope you enjoyed this book and that you will seek your understanding of this discovery.

Brian

17 - Brian Joseph Snyder's Bio

Brian grew up traveling and living in Europe while living a privileged life of private schools and fine dining. He gave little thought to the congenital heart defect that was always going to heal "in a couple of years."

His bright future crashed down at the age of 15; however, when his cardiologist told him that his murmur was permanent that his heart would not last past the age of 25.

Brian shifted his focus from career and relationship to spirituality and healing, in hopes of discovering a sense of immortality that could negate his sense of impending doom.

From Wiccan spell crafters and shamans and various traditions and many spiritual teachers, he invested nearly 30 years of his life chasing teachers and testing spiritual theories.

Brian achieved various degrees of success in his quest but did not appreciate the value of his training until he was forced to endure wildfires that consumed his home and belongings, twice.

While awaiting disaster aid from relief agencies, he realized that he was not upset about the loss. "I felt the tragedy as it happened, and so when it was over, I no longer had to attend to it."

The lack of residual trauma convinced Brian that he had achieved the freedom long sought by many seekers: the freedom to genuinely enjoy life now, unimpeded by memories or latent tendencies.

After several years of teaching his material and streamlining the process, Brian is now sharing his findings with the public.

The YBNL Online "Playshop" is a freely-available video workshop series available at YouTube.com/freeoflimits, while further classes can be found through YourBodyNeverLies.org.

Brian is currently creating an online school and hopes to establish a brick-and-mortar college for personal growth eventually.

Updated
Truth
Can
Serve
You
Best

www.ingramcontent.com/pod-product-compliance
Lightning Source LLC
Chambersburg PA
CBHW050605280326
41933CB00011B/1982